The Voyages of Christopher Columbus

BY STEVEN OTFINOSKI

Table of Contents

Pictures To Think About

GULF OF MEXICO

Florid

Cuba

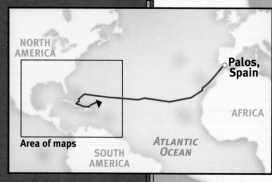

NORTH
AMERICA

Palos,
Spain

AFRICA

Area of maps

ATLANTIC
OCEAN

SOUTH
AMERICA

Central
America

SCALE OF MILES
0   200   400

N
W — E
S

Bahamas

San Salvador

La Navidad •

Hispaniola

Jamaica

Puerto Rico

ATLANTIC OCEAN

CARIBBEAN SEA

South America

Words To Think About

Characteristics

- yearly book
- has information
- ?

almanac

What do you think the word **almanac** means?

Topics

- sun, moon, stars
- weather
- ?

malaria

What do you think the word **malaria** means?

Italian: *mala* (bad)

Italian: *aria* (air)

Read for More Clues

almanac, page 28
colony,   page 8
malaria, page 25

colony

What do you think the word **colony** means in this book?

Meaning 1
a gathering of artists (noun)

Meaning 2
an ant's home (noun)

Meaning 3
a land ruled by a country far away (noun)

Introduction

> **"In 1492, Columbus sailed the ocean blue."**

As the poem says, Christopher Columbus sailed across the Atlantic Ocean in 1492. Columbus was not the first person to discover America. Native peoples had been living in America for thousands of years. Vikings from northern Europe had also landed in America before Columbus. But Columbus did lead the way in exploring America.

Columbus's first voyage, or trip, was very important. He also made three more trips. On each trip he found new things. He visited new lands.

Columbus was born in 1451 in Genoa (JEH-nuh-wuh). Genoa is a city in Italy. His parents were weavers. When Columbus grew up, he wanted to go to sea.

Explorers were looking for a sea route to the Indies. The Indies were islands off the coast of China. Traders brought back spices and gold from the Indies. The only route to the Indies was over land. The land route was slow and costly.

Ships sailed east looking for a sea route. Africa was very big. No one could sail around it. The waters were very dangerous.

It's a Fact

Columbus almost drowned as a young sailor. His ship was attacked by pirates and sunk. He clung to a plank from the ship and swam six miles (9.7 kilometers) to reach shore.

Columbus had an idea. He wanted to sail west. He thought only open water lay between Europe and the Indies. Read on to learn more about Columbus and his voyages.

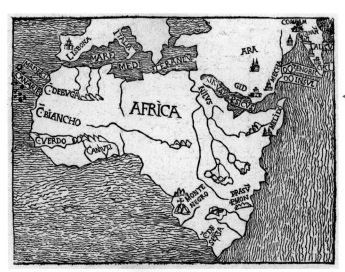

◀ Columbus thought he could sail west from Europe to reach Asia.

Voyage of Discovery

(1492–1493)

▲ No one knows what Columbus really looked like. This portrait, like all the others, was made after his death.

Columbus needed money for his trip. He asked almost every king and queen in Europe for money. They all said no. Finally, Queen Isabella and her husband, King Ferdinand of Spain, said yes. They gave Columbus three ships and a crew of ninety men.

Myth or Reality?

1500s map of a flat Earth

The idea that most people in Columbus's time thought Earth was flat is not true. While some still did, nearly every educated person thought Earth was round. The question was whether it would be possible to get around the planet without running out of food or getting stuck at sea with no wind.

The three ships set sail from Spain on August 3, 1492. They reached the Canary Islands nine days later. There they got more supplies and repaired the ships. Then Columbus headed west into the open ocean.

Into the Unknown

The three ships sailed west for three weeks. They did not see any land. The crew wanted Columbus to turn around and go home. The crew was afraid.

Columbus said if they did not see land in three days, they would go home. A few hours later, they saw signs of land. Birds flew overhead. Branches floated in the sea.

Columbus's Ships

The *Santa Maria* was Columbus's flagship—the one that carried him and flew his flag. This ship was the largest of the three. The *Nina* and the *Pinta* were caravels (KAIR-uh-velz), small, light vessels built for speed. Although he commanded the *Santa Maria*, the *Nina* was Columbus's favorite.

Life on board all three ships was cramped and uncomfortable. There were no steering wheels because they hadn't been invented yet. The ships were steered by a wooden tiller attached to a rudder.

▲ This painting of Columbus's landing at San Salvador hangs in the Capitol Building in Washington, D.C.

A Historic Moment

Early on the morning of October 12, the lookout on the *Pinta* cried "Land! Land!" The sailors landed on a tiny island. Columbus claimed the land for Spain. The natives greeted the sailors.

Columbus named the island San Salvador. It means "Holy Savior." Columbus thought the island was near Japan. It was not. The island is in the Caribbean Sea.

Columbus searched for gold. The only gold he found was in the nose rings worn by the natives.

1. Solve This

Columbus thought the distance from Spain to Japan was 2,500 nautical miles (4,630 km). In fact, the distance is 10,000 miles (18,520 km). How many miles was Columbus off?

Columbus called the natives he met on San Salvador and other islands "Indios" or "Indians." He thought he was near the Indies. He called the islands as a group the West Indies for the same reason. Although he was wrong, the names are still in use today.

Columbus sailed on. Next, he came to a larger island. Columbus thought it was China. It was really the island of Cuba. He looked for gold but did not find any.

Columbus then sailed east. He came upon another large island. He named this island Hispaniola (his-puh-NYOH-luh). Today, this island is divided into two nations. One is Haiti and the other is the Dominican Republic.

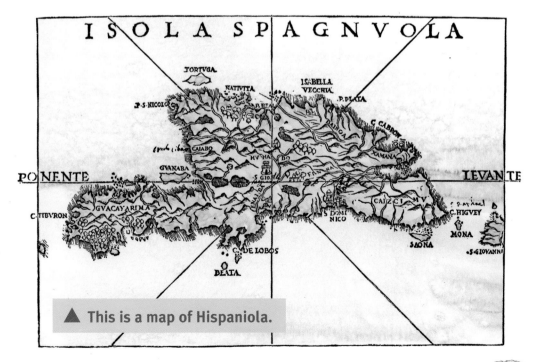

▲ This is a map of Hispaniola.

The First Colony

Columbus explored the coast of Hispaniola. One day the *Santa Maria* hit a **reef**. A reef is a long strip of rock in the water. The ship was wrecked. Columbus decided that this was a good sign. He would start a **colony** (KAH-luh-nee) there.

The men built a fort. They used the wood from the ship. He named the colony La Navidad (LAH nah-vee-DAHD).

Columbus then sailed for Spain with the other two ships. He took six captive Indians with him. He left forty men in the colony. He told them to search the island for gold.

▲ The *Santa Maria* struck a reef while Columbus was exploring the coast of Hispaniola.

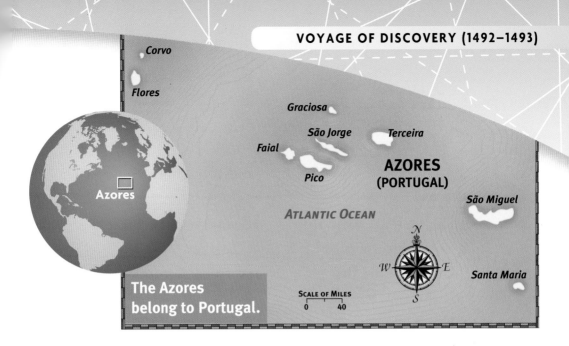

Corvo

Flores

Graciosa

São Jorge   Terceira

Faial

**AZORES
(PORTUGAL)**

Pico

Azores

São Miguel

ATLANTIC OCEAN

N

W   E

S

Santa Maria

**The Azores
belong to Portugal.**

SCALE OF MILES
0   40

Storms at Sea

A huge storm hit the ships on their return trip. The *Nina* almost sank. The men landed on an island. It was one of a group of islands called the Azores (AY-zorz).

The governor thought the men were pirates. He had the men arrested. Columbus was not with them at the time.

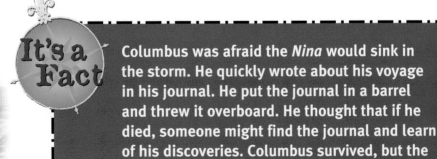

It's a Fact

Columbus was afraid the *Nina* would sink in the storm. He quickly wrote about his voyage in his journal. He put the journal in a barrel and threw it overboard. He thought that if he died, someone might find the journal and learn of his discoveries. Columbus survived, but the barrel was never seen again.

Columbus helped his men. He said he would take over the island if his men were not freed. He also said he would sell all the people on the island into slavery. His threat worked. The men were freed.

The *Nina* and *Pinta* sailed on to Spain. Then another storm hit. The ships had to land in Lisbon, Portugal. While there, Columbus met the king. He showed the king the gold and the captive Indians from the New World.

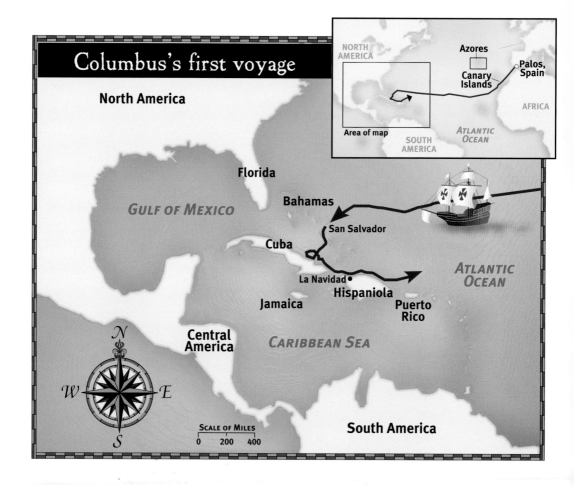

Columbus's first voyage

A Hero's Welcome

Columbus finally landed in Spain on March 15, 1493. He was a hero. He told the king and queen about his travels. He showed them the strange birds, gold masks, and Indians that he had brought back. They named Columbus the Admiral of the Ocean Sea. The Ocean Sea is what people called the Atlantic Ocean long ago.

Columbus made plans for a second trip. It would be much grander than the first. He would still look for a route to the Indies. He would also set up a new colony on Hispaniola.

They Made a Difference

Queen Isabella

Queen Isabella liked Columbus. They both loved adventure and exploring. Isabella's death in 1504 ended Columbus's support at the Spanish court.

11

Grand Voyage

(1493–1496)

Columbus left Spain on his second voyage. He had seventeen ships and 1,200 men. The men were laborers, soldiers, and craftsmen. Craftsmen make things with their hands. These men would help build the colony.

The group also included men who had no skills. These men only came to find gold. They hoped to get rich. There were also six priests and a doctor. The trip took only twenty-one days.

Columbus had fourteen more ships on his second ▲ voyage than he had on his first voyage.

La Navidad

Columbus reached La Navidad on November 22, 1493. He was shocked at what he found. The fort was in ruins. All the colonists were dead or missing. What had happened?

The Indians told him what had happened. The colonists wanted more gold. They fought with the Indians and each other over gold. Finally, the Indians killed the colonists.

Columbus did not punish the Indians. He had promised the king and queen he would be kind to them. Instead, he founded a new colony. He named it Isabella in honor of the queen.

▲ **Columbus reaches the New World.**

Columbus chose a bad place to build the new colony. The land was on a marsh. There were many bugs that spread disease. By summer, many colonists were ill. There was also no gold.

Some of the men did not know how to farm. They wanted to **enslave** the Indians. Then the Indians could farm the land for them.

Columbus wanted to go back to sea. He did not like running the colony. There were too many problems. So Columbus left his brother Diego in charge and went to sea.

New Islands

Columbus explored Cuba. He thought Cuba was part of China. He did not find any spices or gold. Then he went south to what is now the island of Jamaica. The natives there attacked his ship. Again, he could not find gold.

▲ Columbus greets native Cubans.

War on Hispaniola

Columbus sailed back to Hispaniola. The colony was at war. The colonists were fighting the Indians. The colonists wanted Columbus to help enslave the Indians. To keep them happy, Columbus helped the colonists.

Columbus and his soldiers won the war. He captured 1,500 Indians. He sent 500 to Spain to be sold as slaves.

He let the men take the remaining Indians as their slaves. During the time that Columbus lived, many people felt that enslaving Indians was fine.

The Fate of the Arawaks

The Arawak population of Hispaniola was probably about 400,000 when Columbus arrived. By 1531, only about 600 Arawaks were left on the island.

Arawaks not only died in fighting, they died from disease that the Spanish brought to the island.

A New Colony

Columbus left for Spain when the fighting ended. He left his brother Bartolome (bar-TAU-luh-may) in charge. Bartolome started a new colony. He named the colony Santo Domingo.

Columbus Arrives in Spain

Columbus arrived in Spain in March 1496. He had been gone for two and a half years. He was no longer a hero.

Many men had returned before him. These men said he and his brothers were mean and were bad leaders. He had not found the Indies, spices,

It's a Fact Santo Domingo is the capital city of the Dominican Republic. It is the oldest European city in the Western Hemisphere.

▲ Santo Domingo has many historic buildings.

or gold. The king and queen had lost faith in Columbus. Still, they decided to give him another chance.

✓ Point

Talk About It

Imagine you are a colonist on Hispaniola. What would you do to survive? Discuss your ideas with a classmate.

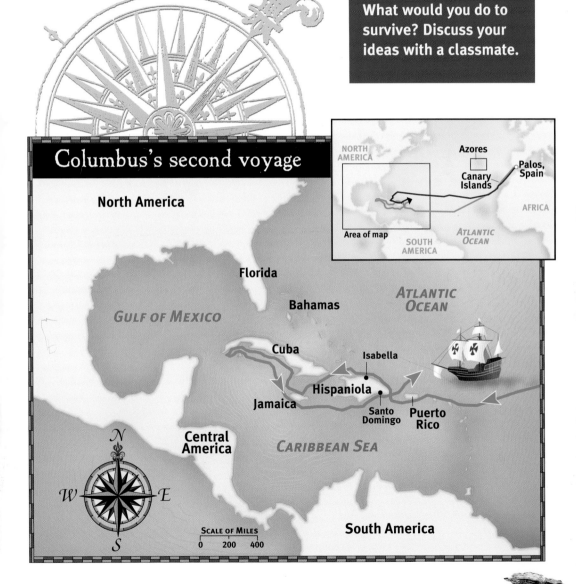

Columbus's second voyage

North America

NORTH AMERICA

Azores

Palos, Spain

Canary Islands

Area of map

AFRICA

ATLANTIC OCEAN

SOUTH AMERICA

Florida

ATLANTIC OCEAN

GULF OF MEXICO

Bahamas

Cuba

Isabella

Hispaniola

Jamaica

Santo Domingo

Puerto Rico

Central America

CARIBBEAN SEA

N
W   E
S

SCALE OF MILES
0   200   400

South America

Unlucky Voyage

(1498–1500)

Columbus had to wait almost two years before he sailed to the New World again. This time he had only four ships. Some of his crew were from prisons. Many men did not want to sail with him. They had heard bad things about Columbus.

He finally left Spain on May 30, 1498. This trip was unlucky. First, he went south. He hoped to reach Japan. This was a mistake.

The part of the sea near the equator is called the **doldrums** (DOLE-drumz). There is little wind there. Ships that use sails to move can get stuck. Columbus's ships did not move for eight days. Finally the winds picked up. The ships moved on.

Columbus Finds South America

Columbus sailed to the island of Trinidad (TRIH-nih-dad). He thought the island was very beautiful. Then he sailed on. He reached more land.

It's a Fact

The doldrums can be very hot. The region is also one of the rainiest in the world. It has sudden and violent thunderstorms.

At first, Columbus thought it was another island. Then he found a very large river. He did not think an island could have such a large river. He called this land "other world." Where was he? It was South America. Columbus was the first European to set foot in South America.

The natives of the land got **pearls** from oysters. Columbus's men wanted to stay and get some gems. But Columbus wanted to keep sailing.

▲ In South America, Columbus discovered pearls. His men traded with the natives for them.

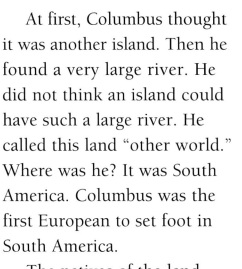

◀ By his third voyage, Columbus was getting old. He had arthritis, a disease that stiffens joints.

Columbus set sail for Hispaniola. The colony was in trouble. Some men did not like Columbus. They joined the Indians and fought the other colonists.

Some people in Spain said Columbus was stealing money and mistreating the colonists. The king and queen wanted to find out what was going on in the colony. They sent a man to Hispaniola. The man's name was Francisco de Bobadilla (frun-SIS-koh deh boh-buh-DEE-yuh).

▼ Columbus is arrested by Francisco de Bobadilla.

Columbus in Chains

Bobadilla arrested Columbus and his two brothers. Bobadilla said they had mistreated the colonists. This was not true. The men were poor leaders, but they had not mistreated anyone. The colonists would not work. The colonists were out of control.

Columbus and his brothers sailed back to Spain in chains. The captain of the ship wanted to take off the chains. Columbus said no. He said only the king and queen could free him.

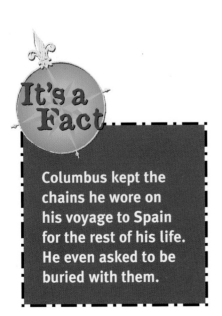

It's a Fact

Columbus kept the chains he wore on his voyage to Spain for the rest of his life. He even asked to be buried with them.

▲ 1881 illustration of Columbus in chains

The king and queen did free Columbus and his brothers. The king and queen did not think the men had mistreated anyone. Still, Ferdinand and Isabella were not happy with Columbus. He still had not found gold or a new route. He promised the king and queen he would. They let Columbus make one last trip.

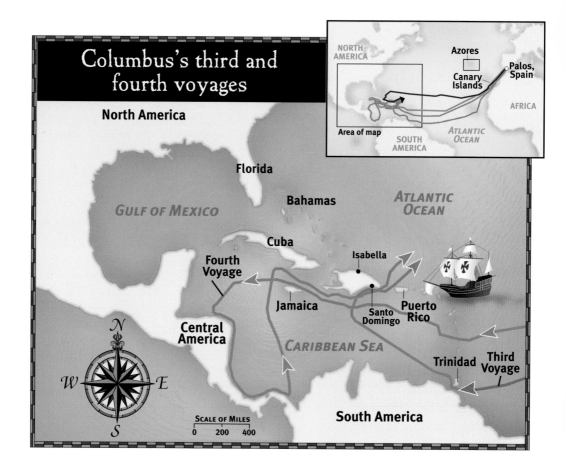

Columbus's third and fourth voyages

Adventurous Voyage

(1502–1504)

Columbus was now fifty-one years old. His crew was very young. Some crew members were only twelve. Others were eighteen. His thirteen-year-old son, Ferdinand, went on the trip.

Columbus had four ships. He wanted to find a route to the East. He hoped to find a route between Cuba and South America. He set sail on May 9, 1502.

2. Solve This

There were 140 members of Columbus's crew on his fourth voyage. About one-third of them were boys aged 12–18. How many of the crew were boys?

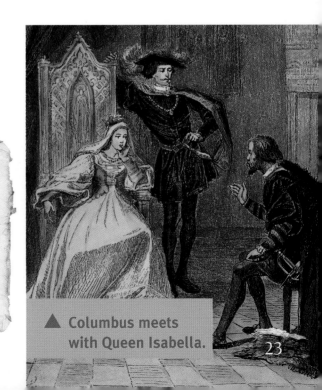

▲ Columbus meets with Queen Isabella.

23

The Hurricane

The king and queen told Columbus not to stop at Hispaniola. Columbus planned to do so anyway. As he got near the island, a huge storm hit. Columbus asked if his ship could come into the port at Santo Domingo. The governor said no.

Columbus sailed farther down the coast. There he brought his ships close to land. He was lucky. The storm did not do much damage to his ships.

▼ Columbus's ships were caught in a bad storm near Santo Domingo.

Search for a Waterway

Columbus next set sail across the Caribbean Sea. He reached some islands off what is now Central America. He sailed up and down the coast. He looked for a waterway to the East. He could not find one.

He did find some gold. He traded goods for the gold.

He wanted to start a colony where gold could be mined. The Indians did not want Columbus and his men there. The Indians killed some of the men. Columbus was now sick. He had a disease called **malaria** (muh-LAIR-ee-uh). He decided to sail for Spain. His ships were in bad shape. He left two of them behind.

Historical Perspective

Columbus came very close to making another great discovery. At one point, he was only about fifty miles (eighty km) from the Pacific Ocean. He had heard from the natives about a great sea to the west. But he decided he didn't have the men or supplies to reach it.

It's a Fact

Governor Ovando sent ships loaded with gold to Spain. Twenty of the ships sank in the hurricane and 500 lives were lost. Among those who died was Columbus's old enemy, Francisco de Bobadilla. The only ship to reach Spain was carrying gold that belonged to Columbus.

Marooned!

The other two ships sailed slowly east. Columbus knew the ships would not make it to Spain. He ordered the crews to land on the coast of Jamaica.

There the men tore the ships apart. None of the men knew how to build another ship. They used the wood to build cabins. Now Columbus and his men were **marooned** (muh-ROOND). They needed to get help. Otherwise, they would never get off the island.

The Indians let Columbus take two canoes. He sent men to get help. The men journeyed 400 miles (640 km). One canoe reached Santo Domingo. The men asked for a ship. The governor would not give them one. The governor was afraid Columbus might come back and take over the island.

Primary Source

Columbus dearly loved his son Ferdinand and was proud of him. Columbus wrote this about his son in his journal: "What gripped me most was the suffering of my son, to think that so young a lad, only 13, should go through so much. But our Lord lent him such courage that he even heartened the rest, and he worked as though he had been to sea all of a long life. That comforted me."

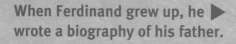

When Ferdinand grew up, he ▶ wrote a biography of his father.

Back in Jamaica, things were going badly. The men were angry. The men blamed Columbus for their troubles.

Some men stole canoes and tried to get to Hispaniola. They didn't make it. When these rebels came back, they fought with the men who had stayed with Columbus. Some of the rebels were killed. When the fighting was over, Columbus did not punish anyone.

Columbus and his men had a bigger problem. The Indians stopped giving the men food. Soon they would starve.

☑ **Point**

Think About It

Do you think Columbus would have been more successful as an explorer if he had realized he was in the Americas and not the East? Why or why not?

This dugout canoe is from present–day Jamaica. ▶

Columbus read his **almanac** (AUL-muh-nak). This book said an **eclipse** (ih-KLIPS) would take place on February 29. Columbus had a plan. He told the Indians to give the men food, or the gods would take away the moon.

The Indians did not believe him. Then, on the night of February 29, the eclipse happened. The moon did disappear. The Indians grew scared. They begged Columbus to help. They would give the men food if he brought back the moon. Columbus said he would help. When the eclipse ended, the moon returned.

▲ Columbus used his knowledge of an upcoming eclipse to get help from the Indians in Jamaica.

The Indians gave the men all the food they wanted after the eclipse happened.

Last Days

The men in Santo Domingo waited seven months for a ship. Finally, the governor gave them one. The men sailed to Jamaica. They picked up Columbus, his son and his brother, and twenty-two others. Then they sailed to Spain. The rest of the crew had to wait for another ship.

Columbus did not see the queen again. She was too sick to see him. She died about a month after he returned. Columbus did see the king. Columbus was rich, but he wanted titles and respect. The king did not grant him any titles. Columbus died on May 20, 1506. It would be several hundred years before he became known as a great explorer.

Why Not Columbia?

Since Columbus "discovered" America, why isn't it named for him? Probably because Amerigo Vespucci (uh-MAIR-ih-goh veh-SPOO-chee) was a better salesman. Vespucci had claimed to sail with another explorer from Portugal to Brazil. Whether he actually did or not is uncertain. But he wrote a book about the adventures that he said he had. The book became a best seller. Soon mapmakers were calling the two new continents America for Amerigo. Columbus hasn't been forgotten. The capital of the United States is named for him. So is the South American country of Colombia.

Conclusion

Columbus discovered hundreds of islands. He was the first European to set foot on Central and South America. But he never understood what he had found. To the day he died, he believed he had found the Indies.

Use the time line to retell the story of Columbus.

The Voyages of Columbus
(1492–1504)

First Voyage

August 3, 1492–March 15, 1493

- Sets sail from Spain
- Founds a colony, La Navidad, on Hispaniola

Second Voyage

September 25, 1493–March 1496

- Founds second colony on Hispaniola at Isabella
- Explores Jamaica and other islands
- Brother Bartolome founds Santo Domingo, a third colony, in 1496

Third Voyage

May 30, 1498–1500

- Explores Trinidad and northern coast of South America
- Is arrested with brothers on Hispaniola and sent back to Spain in chains

Fourth Voyage

May 9, 1502–1504

- Explores coast of Central America
- Is marooned in Jamaica
- Returns to Spain for last time

Glossary

almanac   (AUL-muh-nak) a yearly book that gives information about the stars, moon, sun, tides, and weather (page 28)

colony   (KAH-luh-nee) a territory settled by people from another place (page 8)

doldrums   (DOLE-drumz) an ocean region near the equator where there is little wind (page 18)

eclipse   (ih-KLIPS) the blocking of light passing from one heavenly body to another (page 28)

enslave   (in-SLAVE) to take away a person or people's freedom (page 14)

malaria   (muh-LAIR-ee-uh) a feverish disease transmitted by an insect's bite (page 25)

marooned   (muh-ROOND) left ashore on a deserted place (page 26)

pearl   (PERL) a white, shiny gem that is formed inside some oysters (page 19)

reef   (REEF) a ridge of rocks or coral near the surface of water (page 8)

Index

Solve This

Answers

❶ Page 6 **7,500 miles (13,890 km)**

❷ Page 23 **47 of the crew members were boys**